Stillness After the Rain

Stillness After the Rain

A COLLECTION OF POEMS

ARKA GHOSH

An imprint of
Srishti Publishers & Distributors

Srishti Publishers & Distributors

A unit of AJR Publishing LLP
212A, Peacock Lane
Shahpur Jat, New Delhi – 110 049

editorial@srishtipublishers.com

First published in India by Launchpad,
an imprint of Srishti Publishers & Distributors in 2026

10 9 8 7 6 5 4 3 2 1

Printed and bound in India.

For Maa, Baba and
all the beautiful people I have ever
met in my life....

Contents

Section 1
Nights & Lights

Under the Spring Moon

Walking to a poem party,
beneath the spring moon's glow,
words flutter like leaves,
carried on the breeze of anticipation.
The night hums with verses,
A chorus of hearts beating in ink,
under the celestial sphere,
we find unity in dreams.
Here, beneath the tender gaze of Luna,
emotions paint the night.

Song of the Frost

Upon the frosty bamboo, a heart is heard,
A tiny Bulbul sings, untouched by the cold.
Its notes pierce winter's stark, its song's the word,
A hymn to life whispers bold.
Bamboo branch, nature's cradle, bare yet strong,
Nestles the small, braving winter's long throes.
In frost's bitter bite, a tiny bird's song,
An echo of warmth, life's ember that glows.

Night's Query

In the vastness of the night,
Does my star sleep alone too?
Amid the sprawling canvas of darkness
Besides the river of heaven's embrace.
Each twinkle a silent story,
of vast distances & quiet spaces,
boundless, endless in its expanse,
yet held within the cosmos trace.
Drifting, seeking, always yearning,
Amidst the myriad of celestial lights,
In the river of universe flowing,
Does my star too seek another's sight?

The Moon & the Lamp

In the quiet of midnight's embrace,
The moon whispers secrets to the silent earth,
Illuminating dreams, casting silver on our thoughts
Yet, amidst this lunar dance,
The glare of a neighbour's lamp intrudes,
Bright & unwelcome in its assertion.
It speaks of life's daily bustle,
Interrupting the night's sacred solace,
But even in its interference,
The moon remains patient,
Guiding still, amidst man made luminance,
Always glowing, ever timeless.

Moon & Fireflies

Fireflies in the meadow, tiny lanterns flickering.
Beautiful and purposeful,
against the darkness.
The moon, a constant, unyielding luminescence,
overshadowing these minute sparks.
Yet, in their fleeting moments, fireflies weave
a tapestry as complex
& profound as the moon's own glow.
Both celestial & terrestrial lights, in silent dialogue,
comparing not in size, but in the essence of their light.

Section 2
Changing Seasons

Falling Time

In the quiet pause,
Breath held between seasons,
Earth herself seems to linger
Waiting for gravity's soft pull on amber fragments.
The sky's blue deepens
As if savoring each descending leaf.
Moments stretch,
Like the arc of sun sliding reluctantly below the horizon.
In stillness,
We gather the falling memories
Bearing the weight of impermanence,
cradled in the arms of endless cycles.

Unfolding Autumn

In the shadow of turning elm,
a caterpillar weaves
not yet graced by wings,
as autumn sings its amber hymn.
Yearning fills each fragile segment,
a quiet ache for sky
even as world darkens
with the weight of coming frost.
Is it fear or is it longing
that trembles through its form?
Questions wrapped in silken thread,
a hope that's not yet worn.
The air grows cool, the leaves descend
Still it dreams, against the end.

Autumn Rain

Lamplight,
casting circles on cobblestone,
the autumn rain
a curtain drawn
by an unseen hand.
Glimmering,
a lone beacon holds
against the relentless drip-drip symphony,
a small defiance
in the night's soft sigh.
Each drop's impact
a whispered secret,
the lamplight listens.

Seasons in the Soil

Amidst the drift of time,
In the garden, old hands caress soil—
a sunflower, its head heavy with seeds,
leans into the late summer sun.
Each petal, once vibrant and reaching,
now folds softly toward rest.
Lines map the gardener's face,
grooves deep as the roots
that clutch earth beneath.
Yet, eyes gleam—reflecting skies and seasons,
mirroring the endless cycle.

Seasons of Grace

Autumn, a painter of time,
brushes strokes of gold & rust,
dabs colour where green once stood –
on trees, on the shrivelled leaf at our feet.
This autumn,
with its crisp breath & mellow sun,
lights the room where a mother lies on bed,
her smiles a quiet testament to enduring grace.
In her gaze, a quiet understanding,
as if the cycle of leaf mirrors our own,
gently cradled in the passage of days.

Section 3
Whispers of Nature

Nature's Embrace

When my heart is heavy, laden with dread,
I walk toward the whispering trees
where verdant boughs sway like a cradle
and there, I turn my weary head
A rill runs through, murmuring secrets
in languages only stones and pebbles comprehend.
The sky paints itself in hues of reprieve,
a palette washing over my anxious thoughts.
O, Nature, in your quiet moments
you sing a lullaby for the restless.
I leave lighter, my burdens softened
by the grace of your unfailing embrace.

Violet Vale

In the hush of dawn, brimming with violets,
I wandered to the wild side,
Where whispers of wind told tales,
Of secrets buried deep within the heart,
Of a valley untouched, untamed,
To essence pure, a silent testimony,
To nature's undying vow.
As dusk descended, shadows played,
With colours fading, yet hope remained,
For in this sacred, silent space,
The soul finds, solace and love sustains.

Essence of Dewdrops

In the morning's quiet whisper
dewdrops hang jewel on a spider thread.
Fleeting, fragile,
as if life itself paused, held its breath.
Like those droplets, glistening in times of dawn,
each one of us a world,
carrying reflections of sky, earth, fire, water
the pulse of existence.
Yet we evaporate, absorbed into the air,
the unseen.
And in this vanishing,
dewdrops remind us:
be brilliant, however brief.
Trails of Tranquillity
Nature walk,
beneath the canopy, life beholds.
The trail lit by,
birdsongs, a chorus woven through the air.
With every pace, a soft rustle,
a gentle conversation carried on the wind.
Here, in the unadorned quiet,
where tangled thoughts untwine & drift away,
cradled in the arms of wild
we find our serene, sacred space.
—Welcoming the week on Monday evening.

Garden of Promise

My winter garden,
crammed full,
in every branch, petals, leaves, buds
An embrace of scent & sun.
Shadows shift underfoot,
As light dances unpredictable paths,
The very air seems to breathe,
Saturated with life & promise.
In the hum of bees,
As the frost kissed flower bloomed bright,
Birds, in their cheerful chatter,
Weaving songs between the trees.
—Winter's whisper, in this garden, turns silence into songs.

Section 4
Stars & Dreams

Rain & Midnight Train

I follow the wet solace of the rain,
every droplet a syllable in nature's articulate speech.
Falling on rooftops, whispering soothing songs
to the insomniac hearts below.
Then comes the midnight train,
an echo in the distance, slicing through the night.
With promises of unknown destinations,
it courts my wandering spirit.
Together, rain and train compose
the hymn of my nocturnal soul.
Two fleeting comforts, singing in harmony,
a serenade for those who find solace in the ephemeral.

Lingering Eyes

Waking after a dream,
the room still dim,
colours blend at the edge of sleep
where reality softens.
I remember eyes, the colour of irises,
deep and blooming under twilight's sigh.
They hold the warmth of whispered secrets,
the chill of distant stars.
Morning stirs, light creeps,
and the dream fades—but those eyes linger.

Farewell at Frost's End

As dawn breaks, your whisper floats through the silence,
"Are you finally saying farewell?"
A question hanging in the cold air,
like the last leaf clinging to the bough.
Lingering frost traces patterns on my window,
a testament to the night's we've shared.
Those crystal, a memory in frozen time,
Soon to melt away under the morning's gaze.
But in this moment, between the fading stars
and the first light, we understand the beauty of letting go.

Truth of the Sky

Echoes brush the veil of night,
In the shadowed caress, lies conceal,
hiding nothing except
the truth of the sky.
Beneath the celestial canopy's reach,
Within the silent watch of
—dark woods.
Mysteries hold firm, yet stars unveil,
Bound by time's, fleeting step,
The cosmos & timbered hearts converge.
—Hiding the truth of the sky
—Dark woods.

Sailing Dreams

Setting sail upon the vastness,
Where the horizon touches dreams,
Upon purple clouds, afloat,
Echoes of ancient serenades,
Caressing the canvas of the mind.
The western sea beckons,
A realm of golden dusks,
Where time weaves its own lullaby,
And stars dance on the water's edge.
Embraced by the infinite,
We drift, boundless & free.

Section 5
Silent Thoughts

Threads of Legacy

The Mother's will,
Undulating
In the stillness of her starched saree.
The strength of years,
Between each weave,
Holding more than fabric,
Stories, silent & echoing,
Resilient like edges that never fray,
Emotions cradled in every drape,
Lines of experience,
Her legacy
A touch, a feel, undeniable.

Grounded Wings

In the quiet of the night, perhaps you are a bird
robbed of wings, yet not of song
feathers replaced by whispered words,
plumage lost, but your eloquence strong.
So you dance, on barren ground,
each step a verse, each leap a line.
You've discovered the sky in syllables found,
soaring in stanzas when you can't in time.
They say you're earthbound, a creature confined,
but listen, they know not the hymns you keep.
Your rhythm is air, your cadence is wind,
and in each metaphor, you find your sweep.
Perhaps your wings are thoughts that dare
Maybe you're a bird, still claiming the air.

Shared Shade

In the arbor's tranquil grace,
Sharing tree shade face to face,
With a tiny butterfly
Fluttering near then soaring high.
A friend from a different life,
Unburdened by mortal strife.
Teaching me the art of change,
In a world of both wide and strange
In this evening's sacred hour,
Both aware of nature's power,
We find peace beneath the sky.

Silent Witness

Amidst the rubble
the aftermath of the war gone by,
a doll, unblinking,
still holding.
Still fingers
weathered by time's cruel jest,
touch memories only she knows.
Beneath her gaze,
of loss, of love,
time stands in quiet repose.

Creative Pause

In the weight of stalled creation,
Writer's block cast its shadow.
The pen paused, ink poised, waiting
As ideas ebbed in the shallow.
Yet outside my window frame
The grass grew taller by ten inches,
Nature's script unfurled without fame,
While my thoughts remained in clinches.
For in the dance of words unsaid,
Time, undeterred, moved ever ahead
Tales woven in every wind's knock,
Even when my muse chose to block.
—Last few days in Kandagara.

Section 6
Brief Moments

Stillness after the Rain

After the fall of night rain
A hush cradles the earth
As if the world holds its breath,
Afraid to disturb the quiet.
Moonlight drips from petals to leaf,
A slow cascade of silvery tears,
We are both witness, you & I,
To the silence that speaks louder than words.
In the stillness, even our heart breaks
Become whispers,
Syncing in a rhythm, only we comprehend.
Dreams are but heartbeat away
Floating on night's dark sea.
And as dawn stretches, yawning
Across the sky,
We find ourselves reborn
In the stillness after the storm.

Fading Elegance

In the muted stillness of twilight's descent
Crimson roses, lavender & white
Never looked so alive
As in their impending wither.
Petals, once firm & unyielding,
Now caress the earth like autumn leaves,
Their aroma, stronger, as if screaming life,
Even as they bow to inevitable death.
Yet in these transient moments,
Where life and end dance intimately,
The rose reveals a truth:
Beauty is most poignant in its fragility.

The Gulmohar

Not bothered by what's gone,
or what lies ahead looming.
Amid the turmoil, stands the gulmohar,
In quiet, fiery bloom.
No shackles of yesterday,
Nor dreams of tomorrow's song.
Just the vivid present,
Where blossoms belong.
Simple, Now, Unswayed,
Gulmohar stands alone, undeterred.

Morning's Prelude

Cranky morning awakens
tinged with subtle gray of dawn,
where the world is still half dreaming,
and the air clings with remnants of night.
The radio stirs,
a crackle & snap cutting through silence,
its static whisper a prelude
to the day's unscripted symphony.
In this moment, between sleep & wake,
lies the unspoken poetry of new beginning.

Tulip & Child

Tulip, amidst the carnival din,
Stands
A whisper of nature's art,
Amidst the clamour of spinning wheels & candy hearts.
The pretty flower girl weaves between shouts,
Eye caught by its pull,
In the midst of manmade glee,
In silent, blooming soul calls to she.
In this wild dance of colours & sound,
They find quiet space,
Tulip & child,
Lost & found in a brief embrace.

Section 7
Fleeting Beauty

Flutter & Fall

Blossoms falling, silent, soft,
like whispers they touch the earth,
turning to dust beneath our feet.
Amid the quiet decay,
butterflies dance—
a flutter of wings, a flicker of colour.
They weave through the air,
carefree in their brief brightness,
chasing the sun's warm smile.
All around, life whispers,
in the dance of decay and rebirth,
where every end blooms into a beginning.

Tide & Clover

In the hush of the dawn, the ocean tide whisper
A symphony of small shells, intermingled with clover.
Each wave, a caress, stirs the tender green
As if to remind us, life & love blend seamless.
A salty breeze sweeps over, cradling emotions,
those lost, those found.
They rise & fall, rhythmic as tides.
Yet, here, in the fragility of shells & leaf, equilibrium.
Imagine hearts unfolding like clover petals,
Braving the tidal forces that pull them asunder
In this liminal space
Where water meets earth,
Where feelings meet thought
We find grace.
We become essence: mutable, yet everlasting.
In the dance of shell & clover, we find our tide.

Dragonfly Days

In the waning light
the day slips through our fingers
like water, clear & rushing,
as if the life of the dragonfly,
brief yet brilliant in its flight.
Skimming over the pond's mirrored surface
It dances, a fleeting gem in fading sunlight.
Every flutter of its thin wings,
a soft murmur in the calm of the evening
a tribute to the beauty of the transient
the art of living fiercely within the confines
of a moment, always precious, always brief.

Winter Sky

Stiller than stillness,
the winter sky stretches,
a canvas untouched by brushstrokes,
cold, vast
unbroken.
Shadows of trees reach out,
touching nothing but chill.
No bird dares break its silence,
no wind whispers its secret.
Between breaths of the Earth,
the heart of the world rests,
in the frozen expanse
of the winter sky.

Morning Sun

Golden threads of daybreak,
push against the veil of dawn
slipping, sneaking, finding paths
through the slenderest of window gaps.
Morning sun,
Persistent & silent,
carves warmth in the chill of leftover night,
an insistent invader of shadow realms.
And as the room bathes
in this gentle intrusion,
all that is hidden
meets the promise of a new day.

Section 8
Heartfelt Stories

Red Roses Remember

Today I break my resolve
to never write about you
among red roses, I remember
how their thorns caught our laughter.
Simple petals, they unfold
like the days we dared to dream
beneath a sky too wide to hold
all our whispers and our screams.
Now, each bloom is a verse
of love, of pain, entwined
red roses remind me—
you, I cannot leave behind.

Love's Uncharted Caverns

In the silent weight of love's transaction,
Beyond measure,
More than coins or paper tallies,
The heart offers up its tributes,
Its depths,
Its uncharted caverns.
The marketplace of emotions never balances,
Yet we pay,
Often beyond our means,
For love's intangible essence,
Unaffordable,
Yet given freely.

Dreams in Bloom

Our dreams, wild flowers in the heart's deep soil,
Spring up where least we guess, a surprise.
They print dull life with colours,
Lighting up the barren lands, dispelling gloom.
In nooks of thoughts, in corner dark & bare,
They scatter seeds of joy.
Despite life's winter harsh & cold despair.
In dreams we find our strength, our inner light.

Butterfly Inquiry

Little butterfly,
perched on the edge of a petal,
let me ask you about poetry.
Do your wings whisper verses
when they brush against the morning dew?
Is there rhythm in your flight,
synced to the heartbeat of the sun?
Tell me,
how each flutter pens a stanza
in the air,
so effortlessly.

Section 9
Echoes of Everyday

Market Days

Market day stirs,
The farmer's horse, a steady drum
Barefoot steps, voice merge
The oomph, palpable in the morning hum.
Amongst stalls and barter's dance,
Life unfolds in every glance—
The village, the crowd, the horses & the rhymes.

Bread and Tears

In the cramped alley, she sobs—
her tears mingling with the dust,
a beggar woman, trembling hands
raise and fall, with each thud
a piece of her own heart bruises.
Her child, small and scared,
clutches a stolen loaf—
eyes wide, understanding nothing
but hunger and now, this sharp love.
She cries for him, for herself,
for their world so cruelly hollow—
where bread is a treasure, too precious, too rare.

Tea & Roses

Yellow roses,
Unfurling in the quiet hum of dawn,
Fragrances of roasting tea leaves,
Weave through the air, a soft, persistent song.
No rhymes to bind, nor meter to confine,
Just the earth, the blooms, the steam, intertwining.
Here, in the simplicity of scent & sight,
we find the pulse of day & the calm of night.
—Days in Bengaluru, Bende Kaalu Uru, the town of
boiled beans.

A Coastal Village

In a coastal village,
where all roads run
to the sea,
life moves
to the rhythm of tides.
An old fisherman mends nets—
hands woven with the lines of his craft,
eyes reflecting the vast, open waters.
Children laugh,
their feet bare and hearts wild,
chasing the whispers of the ocean,
as the sun dips low—
every path leading home,
cradling us back to the sea's soothing arms.

Voice of Soul

In sun ray's warmth, in droplet's playful song,
Amidst the wind that whispers tales untold,
A soul that savours earth's perfume so strong,
Is one that truly grasp life's thread of gold.
For he who seizes moments, pure and whole,
Discerns the voice of soul in every fold.

Section 10
Paths and Reflections

Solitary Voyage

Alone, a boat on a boundless sea,
Unfettered, free, as one could be.
Solitude its only company,
Echoing silence in harmony.
Drifting on waves, beneath vast sky,
Underneath the moon's watchful eye.

Lost Roads Home

In the hush of twilight embrace,
Find me where the lost souls linger,
Between the shadows & glow,
At the end of a lonesome road.
Whisper of ancient tale retold,
Where the wild ones dance, unbridled,
Moonlight brushes against my skin,
And the stars, they serenade my spirit.
In this realm, untamed & unknown,
Hear the melody of cosmic sigh,
For its haunting tune & tone,
The music calls me home.

Joyful Sparrow

In the alley's quietude,
a sparrow rejoices
nourishment discovered on weathered steps.
No grand feast, yet it dances,
tiny feet in rapture
over humble offerings.
Beyond the door, lives clutter,
hearts burdened by abundance.
Yet here, joy distilled in simplicity.
Unseen, but echoing
the winged one's jubilant hymn
to life's minor miracles.

Quiet Water

In the hushed domain of timeless water,
—old pond,
Reflecting a world of softened hues,
An egret, still as the space between breaths,
Rivalling the stillness,
Of time's slow crawl.
Murmur of lily pads & darting fish,
Echoes of a world pristine,
By man's hastened pace,
...nature's tranquil tableau.

Still on a Journey

At the end of a long dream,
Whispers of distant landscapes,
Echoes of times past caress,
Journeys taken, path crossed,
Footprints on the canvas of eternity.
Yet here I stand,
In the ever-shifting sand of memory,
The weight of eons in my eyes,
Yet the lightness of a moment on my lips.
And the stillness of the now,
The heart confirms what the soul already knows,
Still alive,
On a journey.

Acknowledgements

My heartfelt gratitude begins with **The Book Bakers** agency, and especially Mr. Suhail Mathur, for their instrumental role in bringing this collection to Srishti Publishers & Distributors.

Their belief and guidance have been pivotal in this journey. I extend my sincere thanks to **Srishti Publishers & Distributors** – particularly Mr. Arup Bose and the entire team – for welcoming me into the Srishti family. Their support in publishing my debut collection, has been invaluable.

The timeless wisdom of Rumi and the ever-present beauty of Nature have been profound inspirations for many of these poems.

And to the many inspiring souls who have crossed my path, whose presence and spirit have unknowingly shaped these verses.

Thank you. This journey would not have been the same without each of you.